Sunday Jones
(Photo by: Hope D. Rugley)

Dedication

To my mother's for never telling me I couldn't do a thing.
To the ones who've had to be strong for too long.
To the ones still figuring it out.
To those who've lost themselves and are still choosing to find themselves again. This is for every soul that's been cracked open but never broken.
For every version of me I had to become, forgive, and love along the way.
And for every version of you still rising.

May these pages hold you when the world doesn't.
May you remember:
You don't have to be perfect to be powerful.
You just have to keep becoming.

This is not just poetry. This is a mirror. A moment. A map.

The Art of Rising: A Love Letter to My Becoming is a soul-soothing collection of affirmations and poems designed to walk with you through healing, self-discovery, grief, and growth. Whether you're at your breaking point or your breakthrough, these words will meet you where you are—and love you there.

Sunday Jones writes with the voice of a warrior, the wisdom of a healer, and the heart of someone who's been through it. Every poem is a reminder:

You are not behind.
You are not broken.
You are not alone.

You're just becoming.
And there's an art to that.

Author Bio :

Sunday Jones writes from the trenches and the triumph. A storyteller at heart, she weaves healing, wisdom, and affirmation into every line. Her purpose is to remind others of their own—because we all deserve a quiet rise and a powerful return to self.

She is a poet, life coach, and voice for the resilient. Through affirmations, storytelling, and spiritual truth, she helps others rise into alignment with who they truly are. Her journey is proof that becoming is a sacred process —and love, the greatest lesson of all.This is her love letter to her own becoming—and to yours.

Introduction

This book was never meant to fix you.
Because you were never broken.

It was written to remind you of your strength.
To whisper to you in the quiet moments.
To scream with you in the dark ones.
To stand beside you in the rising.
Some of these poems were born in the fire.
Others in deep reflection.
But all of them are pieces of my becoming—
and I hope they walk with you in yours.

Read them out loud.
Write them on your mirror.
Pass them to a friend.
Keep them close.
Because the world will try to make you forget who you are.
But these words? They're here to help you remember.

Table of Contents

I. You Are Not Behind

You are not late.
Not lost.
Not lacking.

The road you walk is yours—
paved with purpose,
even when it winds too much
or the signs go missing.

You are not behind.
You are becoming.
And the becoming
takes time.

Let them rush.
Let them race.
You are steady
in your grace.

Even pauses are progress.
Even rest is a kind of rebellion
against the voice that says
"you should be further."

You're exactly where growth can find you.
Exactly where love can reach you.
Exactly where healing begins.

Affirmation:
I am on time for my journey. I trust my pace and honor my path. I trust myself, my instincts and my intuitions.

Seriously,

You've got this , no matter what it is you can get through it, and when you feel like you can't talk to God. Write it down. Talk to the ancestors, a friend that will just listen and not judge. Hey you can call me. You will get through. You've got this. You have a spotter.

2. Bloom Where You're Planted

This soil may not be soft,
but you've still found a way to grow—
through concrete, through chaos,
through every "no" that was meant to crush you.

Still, you stand.
Not always loud, but always real.
Not always ready, but always willing.
You've bloomed in the shadows.
You've made beauty out of survival.
And that,
that is a miracle they won't always recognize.

But you were never waiting for them.
Your roots run deeper than doubt.
Your petals stretch beyond permission.

So bloom.

Right here.
Right now.
Even if it's not perfect.
Even if it's not pretty.

Bloom anyway.

Affirmation:
I am growing in grace, no matter the ground. I bloom where I stand.

I am Blooming
into my existence because, I do exist.

3. The Mirror Isn't Lying

Look again.
Not with the eyes that have been taught
to spot every flaw,
but with the soul that remembers
what you survived to get here.

That face holds stories,
that body holds strength,
those eyes have seen the worst
and still seek the light.
Don't shrink in the reflection.
Don't let the world's weight
make you question your own worth.

The mirror isn't lying—
you are still art.
Still divine.
Still becoming
something powerful.

Speak love into the reflection
until it speaks it back.
Be the kindest voice
your own ears hear.

Affirmation:
I see myself with love. I honor the strength in my
reflection. I love every inc of myself.

4. Healing Is Not Linear

Some days it stings.
Some days it soothes.
Some days you're flying high—
others, you're back in the storm
wondering if you've healed at all.

But this?
This is still healing.

The tears you cried last night
were part of the cleansing.
The silence you needed
was part of the process.
The space you took for yourself
was sacred.

Healing is not a straight line.
It loops. It dips. It spirals.
But every breath, every boundary,

every broken pattern you walk away from—
that's proof.

You're not failing.
You're feeling.
You're facing what once broke you
with open eyes and a braver heart.

Let the journey be messy.
Let it be yours.
You are not behind.
You are healing.

Affirmation:
I honor my healing, even when it hurts. I am not
broken—I am becoming whole.

5. I Forgive Myself Again

I've carried guilt like a second skin—
tight, uncomfortable,
but somehow familiar.

I've replayed the moment,
the words,
the silence,
the mistake.
Again. And again.
But it doesn't change it.
It only drains me.

So today—again—
I forgive myself.

Not because I forgot.
But because I remember who I was
when I did what I did.
I remember the pain I was in.

The fear I was hiding.
The love I was craving.

And I choose compassion.
For that version of me.
For the mess I made.
For the lesson I learned.

Forgiveness is a daily choice.
And I will keep choosing it—
until I feel light again.

Because I deserve that.
Because I am not my past.
Because I have already paid enough
in sleepless nights
and second guesses.

I do not have to carry the weight forever.
I do not have to make myself small
to prove I've changed.

I release it now.
I let it go.

I forgive myself—again.

Affirmation:
I release what I cannot change. I forgive myself with grace and love.

6. Softness Is Strength

They told you to toughen up.
To bite your tongue.
To armor your heart
before this world could wound it.

But you—
you chose softness anyway.

You chose to feel it all.
To cry when it hurt.
To speak when it mattered.
To love when it wasn't returned.

That's not weakness.
That's power.

Softness is standing in the fire
without letting it harden your soul.
It's walking through chaos

and still pausing to notice the light.
Still offering grace.
Still believing in love.

Your softness is resistance—
to the numbness,
to the cruelty,
to the silence that tries to swallow truth whole.

You are a quiet storm,
gentle but grounded.
You are the calm after the wreckage,
the whisper that wakes the sleeping heart.
They won't always understand you.
But that doesn't mean you should change.
The world needs softness
just as much as strength—
and in you, they live as one.

Softness does not mean surrender.

It means holding space.
It means standing firm in who you are without turning cold.

So be soft.
Be strong.
Be exactly who you were meant to be.

Affirmation:
My softness is not weakness. I lead with love, and I am powerful in my peace.

7. Grief Is Love With No Place to Go

It hits out of nowhere—
a song,
a smell,
a memory too loud to ignore.

And just like that,
you're back in that space
where the loss lives.
Heavy.
Uninvited.
Unrelenting.

They told you time would help.
And it has,
but only sometimes.
Because grief isn't something you finish—
it's something you carry.

You carry it in the way
you still set a plate out,
still talk to them in silence,
still dream of the sound of their laugh.

It doesn't mean you're stuck.
It means you loved deeply.
It means your heart remembers.

Grief is the echo of love
that had nowhere else to land.
And that love still lives—
in you,
in the stories you tell,
in the tears you allow to fall.
Don't rush the healing.
Don't shame the ache.
You are allowed to miss them,
even on your best days.
Especially on your best days.

Because their absence shaped you.
But so did their presence.
Hold both.
Honor both.

You will not forget them.
Not today.
Not ever.

Affirmation:
My grief is sacred. I give myself space to feel and grace to heal.

8. Unlearning Is a Victory

You thought you had to be perfect.
To please.
To perform.
To always say "yes" even when your soul screamed
"no."

You were taught that love was earned,
that worth had conditions,
that boundaries were betrayal.

But you know better now.
And even though it's hard—
you're unlearning.

Unlearning the lies that told you
you had to shrink to be accepted.
That your voice was too loud.
Your dreams too big.
Your needs too much.

You are peeling back layers
that were never yours to wear.
You are rewriting your truth
with every "no" you say in peace,
with every "yes" that feeds your joy.

This is victory—
not in battle,
but in becoming.

You are not broken.
You are brave.
You are not difficult.
You are discovering.

And the work you're doing
to heal what they never did—
that's legacy work.
That's freedom work.
You are not a prisoner of your past.
You are the architect of your future.

Affirmation:
I release what no longer serves me. Unlearning is part of my healing.

9. They Didn't Break You

They tried to silence you.
Tried to twist your truth,
dim your light,
turn your softness into shame.

They saw your power
and mistook it for weakness.
But you?
You are still here.
Still rising.
Still radiant.
They threw shade,
but you became your own sun.
They whispered doubt,
but you answered with presence.

No matter what they did—
you remained.

You turned pain into purpose.
Turned wounds into wisdom.
Turned your "why me?"
into "watch me."

You are not who they said you were.
You are not defined by their projections.
You are not the story they wrote.

You are the author now.
And the pen is in your hands.
So write loudly.
Live boldly.
And remind yourself:

They didn't break you.
They couldn't.
You're made of something sacred.

Affirmation:

I am unshaken. I rise beyond the harm. I reclaim my power.

10. Stillness Is Sacred

The world moves fast.
Always rushing,
always reaching,
always demanding.

But you don't have to keep up
with chaos.
You don't have to burn out
to be seen.

There is power in the pause.
In the deep breath.
In the choice to rest.

Stillness isn't laziness—
it's listening.
It's checking in with your spirit
before the world gets too loud.

Stillness is where answers arrive.
Where your heart catches up to your hustle.
Where you remember who you are
without all the noise.
Sit with yourself.
Even when it's uncomfortable.
Even when the silence feels too big.

There is wisdom in the quiet.
And peace in the presence.

You don't always need a plan.
Sometimes, you just need to be.
To exist.
To feel.
To breathe.

Stillness is sacred.
And so are you.

Affirmation:
I honor the stillness. I find peace in presence and power in pause.

11. Speak Like You Matter

Your voice is not too loud.
Your truth is not too much.
Your words were never meant
to be swallowed whole.

You've been taught to shrink—
to weigh every sentence,
to soften every "no,"
to wait for permission.

But no more.

Speak like you matter.
Because you do.

Say what you mean,
without dressing it up
to make it easier for them to digest.

Your truth is not a burden.
It is a gift.

Let your voice be a mirror
for those who have lost their own.
Let it be a home
for those still searching.
Let it be yours—
unapologetic and undeniable.

You do not have to prove your worth
to be worthy of being heard.
You do not have to ask
to take up space.

Your voice is power.
Your words are necessary.

Say them.
Own them.Let the world adjust.
Affirmation:

My voice is powerful. I speak my truth with confidence and clarity.

12. Reclaim Your Name

They called you everything but whole.
Everything but worthy.
Everything but loved.

They labeled you with their fears,
their failures,
their misunderstandings—
but none of it was yours to hold.

You are not broken.
You are not unworthy.
You are not the weight of their words.

You are a masterpiece in motion.
You are the name you choose for yourself.

So reclaim it.

Say it with love.
Say it with pride.
Say it with the power of every ancestor
who refused to be erased.

Your name carries history.
Your name carries hope.
Your name carries you.

And no one else gets to define it.

Affirmation:

I define myself. My name, my story, my truth belong
to me.

13. This Body Is Home

Not a battleground.
Not a burden.
Not a problem to be fixed.

This body—
your body—
is home.

It holds you.
Carries you.
Speaks to you in ways
the world never taught you to hear.

Love it.
Not just when it looks how they say it should.
Not just when it moves the way you want it to.
Love it because it is yours.

Because every scar is a survival story.
Every stretch mark is proof you grew.
Every breath is a blessing.

Your body deserves tenderness.
Your body deserves rest.
Your body deserves to be treated
with the same kindness
you offer everyone else.

Affirmation: I honor my body as my home. I treat it with love and gratitude.

14. Take Up Space

You were not made to be small.
To squeeze yourself
into someone else's comfort.
To apologize for the way you shine.

You are meant to take up space.
To walk into rooms
without questioning if you belong.
To speak,
to stand,
to exist fully.
Do not shrink.
Do not fold yourself into corners
to make others feel bigger.

Stretch out.
Expand.
Be seen.

You are here.
And that is enough.

Affirmation:
I am worthy of space. I exist boldly and without
apology.

15. You're Doing the Work

You may not see it yet,
but it's happening.
The healing.
The growing.
The shifting.

Every small step counts.
Every hard truth faced.
Every old pattern unlearned.

Give yourself credit.
This journey is not easy,
but you're walking it anyway.

You are proof that change is possible.
That healing is real.
That effort, even on the hardest days,
is never wasted.

You are the person you once prayed to become.
You are the evidence of your own transformation.

So don't dismiss your progress
just because you haven't reached the finish line.
There is no finish line—
only deeper healing,
deeper understanding,
deeper love for yourself.

The work is not in being perfect.
The work is in choosing to show up,
again and again,
for yourself.

And you are doing that.
You are doing the work.
And that is enough.

Affirmation:I honor my progress. Every step I take is a step toward healing.

16. Let It Fall Away

Everything that no longer fits—
let it go.

The guilt.
The expectations.
The need to explain yourself
to those who never tried to understand.

Let it fall away.

Not all things are meant to be held.
Not all people are meant to stay.

There is no shame in outgrowing what once felt like
home.
No guilt in setting boundaries
where chaos used to live.

You are allowed to evolve.
You are allowed to move forward.

Let the past be what it was.
Let yourself be who you are now.
Release what weighs you down
so you can rise into what's waiting

Affirmation:
I release what no longer serves me. I trust the
unfolding of my journey.

17. Affirm Your Becoming

Speak life into yourself.
Not just in the good moments,
but especially in the ones
where doubt whispers the loudest.

Affirm your becoming.
Say it like you mean it:

I am growing.
I am healing.
I am worthy of love.
Even on the hard days,
especially on the hard days.

You are not just surviving.
You are stepping into a version of yourself
that is braver,
bolder,
more aligned than ever before.

Affirm that.
Claim that.
Become that.

Affirmation:
I affirm my growth, my healing, and my worth every day.

18. You're Allowed to Rest

Not every battle needs you today.
Not every call deserves an answer.
Not every moment
has to be productive.

Rest is not a reward.
It's a requirement.

You are allowed to pause.
To take a breath.
To simply be.
The world will not crumble
if you close your eyes for a while.
Your worth is not measured
by how much you do,
but by how deeply you honor yourself.

So rest. Guilt-free.

Affirmation:

I honor my need for rest. My worth is not tied to my productivity.

Remember :

Sometimes we think we are going to miss something when the truth is if we don't rest we will miss a lot. Don't be afraid to take care of you.

Be sure to replenish all of the love you dished out to everyone so you can keep going in peace.

19. Fear Can't Drive This Time

Fear has had its hands on the wheel
for too long.

It kept you from speaking.
Kept you from starting.
Kept you in places
that no longer fit you.

Not anymore.

Fear can sit in the back.
It can watch,
it can whisper,
but it does not get to steer.

You are driving now.

Move toward what calls you,
even if your hands shake.

Move toward what sets your soul on fire,
even if your voice trembles.

Fear is not the enemy.
Staying stuck is.

So drive.
Forward.
Free.

Affirmation:
I move beyond fear. I trust my path and take control
of my journey.

20. Loving Yourself Louder

You spent years loving others louder
than you loved yourself.
Pouring, giving, sacrificing.

Now it's your turn.

To choose yourself.
To speak to yourself with kindness.
To show up for your own heart.

Loving yourself loudly
is not selfish.
It is necessary.

Be the love
you so freely give to others.

Affirmation:
I love myself deeply. I honor my needs and my heart.

21. Return to Peace

No matter the chaos around you,
you can always return to peace.

Not by force,
not by control,
but by release.

Breathe deep.
Come home to yourself.

Let the world do what it does.
But let your spirit stay still.

I returned to peace

like a child running home barefoot,

tired of the noise,

craving the hush of my mother's voice

in a language that only my soul remembered.

I traded survival for stillness,

scarred hands finally releasing

what they were never meant to hold.

I no longer chase love

I became it.

Wore it in the silence between breaths,

danced with it in empty rooms,

and prayed it over wounds

I stopped trying to hide.

I returned to peace

not because life stopped hurting,

but because I started listening

to what the hurt was trying to teach.

I made a home inside myself

planted gardens in the ruins,

let the weeds speak their truth

before pulling them gently

at the root.

Peace didn't come all at once—

it tiptoed in like a friend

I had forgotten how to trust.

But I let her stay.

Set an extra plate.

And made space

for her to bloom.

Now, I rest without guilt.

I speak without shrinking.

I rise without apology.

And every time the world tries

to unmake me,

I return to peace—

the soft place

that remembers who I am when I forget.

Affirmation:
I am peace. I return to my center with ease.

22. Not Everyone Gets It, and That's Okay

Some people will never understand you.
And that's okay.

You do not have to explain your magic
to those who refuse to see.

Live anyway.

Be who you are,
not who they expect you to be.

Not everyone gets it,

and that's okay.

Some people only see you

from the version they met,

not the soul that kept rising

even when no one was watching.

They don't understand

why you laugh quieter now,

why you move slower,

why your fire don't burn to prove—

just to warm those who know how to tend it.

You used to beg to be seen.

Now, you bless the ones who do

and release the rest

without bitterness.

You don't show up everywhere

because your spirit no longer fits

in places built on empty praise

and loud performances.

Not everyone gets

why you had to leave,

why you had to heal out loud,

why you're not available

for guilt trips or gaslighting.

And still—

you rise soft.

You rise whole.

You rise free.

They don't have to get it.

They weren't called to it.

You were.

So you walk your road,

barefoot if you have to,

with grace in one hand

and boundaries in the other.

Because peace is a privilege

you paid for in tears,

and now you protect it

like the sacred thing it is.

Not everyone gets it.

And that's the part

you're finally at peace with.

Affirmation:
I am not for everyone, and that is my power.

23. Sacred in the Struggle

Even in the struggle,
there is something sacred.
Something forming,
something strengthening.

You will look back
and see it all made sense.

Keep going.
Your breakthrough is on the other side.
I found the sacred in the struggle.

Not after, not beyond

right in the thick of it.

In the days I didn't want to get up

but did.

In the tears I wiped

before anyone saw them.

In the prayers I whispered

when I didn't have the words,

only the will.

There was divinity in the doubt.

Grace in the grind.

I didn't need a mountaintop

to meet God—

the valley was holy too.

I learned that healing isn't always pretty,

but it's always worth it.

That survival was my first language,

but peace—

peace is what I was born to speak.

I stopped apologizing

for how long it's taken.

I celebrated the crawl

just as loud as the leap.

Because every scar has a scripture,

and I've started to read mine out loud.

This struggle,

it baptized me.

Not in fire,

but in the unrelenting belief

that I could make it through.

And I did.

And I am.

Still rising,

still soft,

still sacred—

even in this stretch of becoming.

So if you see me quiet,

just know I'm listening.

If you see me smiling,

just know I earned it.

If you see me shining,

just know it's not without shadow.

I found the sacred in the struggle.

And now I wear it

like armor.

Like prayer.

Like truth.

Affirmation:
My struggles shape me, but they do not define me.
I honor my journey, even the parts that tried to
break me.

There is divinity in my healing, purpose in my pain,

and strength in every step I take forward.

I am sacred, even in the struggle.

Especially in the struggle.

Stay True,

Just because people put their expectations on you. It does not mean you have to receive them.

You are who you are, so be that not them. I'm not saying don't take advice. I'm saying, stay true to who you are in love and light. Don't let others push them on you.

Don't force what doesn't fit period.

24. Don't Shrink. Shine.

You were not made for dimming.
You are meant to shine.
Step forward.
Be seen.
Own your light.

You don't need permission
to take up space.

Shine because it's who you are.

Don't shrink.

You weren't made for corners.

You weren't born to dim your light

so others could stay comfortable

in their shadows.

Don't fold yourself small

to fit into boxes

you were never meant to occupy.

You are the room.

You are the presence.

You are the pulse that shifts atmospheres.

They'll call you too much—

too loud,

too bold,

too you.

Let them.

You were never meant to be a whisper

in a world that needs your roar.

You survived the silence

just to find your voice again.

Now use it.

Speak in full color.

Walk like you've met the God within you.

Shine like the sun took lessons

from your glow.

Because shrinking never saved you.

It only delayed your freedom.

But shining?

Shining sets generations free.

Shining shows the way.

Shining honors every version of you

that didn't think they'd make it this far.

So take up space.

In rooms, in hearts,

in the pages of your own story.

Be light unapologetically.

Let your brilliance be your boundary.

And if they ask you to quiet down

sing louder.

Laugh bigger.

Shine anyway.

Affirmation:

I am not too much—

I am just enough to move mountains.

I will not shrink to be accepted.

I will shine because I was born to.

My light is necessary,

and I no longer ask for permission to glow.

I shine fully and without apology.

25. It Was Always You

All the strength.
All the wisdom.
All the love you've searched for—
it was always in you.
You are enough.
You always were.
No need to seek outside
what was inside you all along.

Trust yourself.
Believe in yourself.
It was always you.
Don't shrink.

You weren't made for corners.

You weren't born to dim your light

so others could stay comfortable

in their shadows.

Don't fold yourself small

to fit into boxes

you were never meant to occupy.

You are the room.

You are the presence.

You are the pulse that shifts atmospheres.

They'll call you too much—

too loud,

too bold,

too you.

Let them.

You were never meant to be a whisper

in a world that needs your roar.

You survived the silence

just to find your voice again.

Now use it.

Speak in full color.

Walk like you've met the God within you.

Shine like the sun took lessons

from your glow.

Because shrinking never saved you.

It only delayed your freedom.

But shining?

Shining sets generations free.

Shining shows the way.

Shining honors every version of you

that didn't think they'd make it this far.

So take up space.

In rooms, in hearts,

in the pages of your own story.

Be light unapologetically.

Let your brilliance be your boundary.

And if they ask you to quiet down

sing louder.

Laugh bigger.

Shine anyway.

Affirmation:

I am not too much—

I am just enough to move mountains.

I will not shrink to be accepted.

I will shine because I was born to.

My light is necessary,

and I no longer ask for permission to glow.

Everything I need is already within me. I am enough.

Closing Reflections

If you made it to this page, know this:
You are not the same person you were when you
started.
Not because these words changed you—
but because you showed up for you.

That's the real art of rising.
Choosing you.
Again.
And again.
And again.

Don't stop becoming.
Your soul will thank you.

Journaling
&
Reflection Prompts

"Pages for My Becoming"

1. Who was I before the world told me who to be?
Write about your earliest memories of yourself—
before the labels, before the expectations.

2. What parts of me, am I ready to forgive?
List what you're still holding against yourself. Then
speak to those parts with compassion.

3. What does rising look like for me right now?
Is it rest?
Is it starting something new?
Is it walking away from something?
Define what "rising" means in this season.

4. Write a love letter to your current self.
Not who you're becoming. Not who you were. But
the you reading this right now.

5. What am I grieving that I haven't fully given space to?
Write it out. Say its name. Let it know it's okay to be felt, but not forever.

6. What beliefs about myself am I ready to unlearn?
Write the lies first. Then cross them out. Rewrite the truth underneath.

7. I feel most aligned when...
Describe what peace feels like in your body. In your routines. In your spirit. Let this be your reminder.

8. What have I survived that deserves to be honored?
This is not about pain glorification—it's about recognizing your power.

9. Write a letter to your future self.
Speak as if it already happened. "I'm proud of you for..."
Let it be a vision. Let it be a prophecy.

10. What does "Remember Your Dopeness" mean to me?
Take the quote. Make it your own. What makes you powerful, beautiful, divine, and whole? List it. Feel it.

A Love Note to the Reader

Dear Beautiful Soul,

You didn't need this book to be powerful—

you already are.

But if these pages helped you hear your own voice more clearly,

or stand a little taller in your truth,

then it's done what it was meant to do.

This book was a mirror and a microphone.

A quiet conversation between your soul and your becoming.

Each line was a soft reminder:

You are worthy of rising.

You are allowed to rest.

You are built to heal.

Every word was written with intention

for the nights you felt unseen,

for the mornings you didn't feel strong enough to rise,

and for the quiet victories only you know about.

This is your reminder that you are worthy of softness,

and bold enough for greatness.

That your healing is your art.

Your journey is your masterpiece.

And your rise—

your rise is holy.

So whether you're still breaking through,

or finally breathing on the other side of the storm—

please remember:

You are not behind.

You are not too late.

You are not too broken.

You are blooming.

You are learning.

You are coming home to you.

This isn't the end—

it's a beautiful beginning.

Keep rising.

With love and belief in all you are,

Sunday Jones

AKA

Mother Earth on the vibe line (TAG)

Final Affirmation: Check-In, Not Check-Out

I will not check out of myself.

I check in.

Not just to survive, but to be present in my becoming.

To feel what's real, even when it's raw.

To stand at the altar of my own breath and say:

"I am still here. And that matters."

I check in.

With my heart. My spirit. My dreams.

I don't run from the parts of me that ache.

I hold them close, like old friends needing rest.

I don't fake peace—I find it.

I don't numb pain—I name it, and then I rise anyway.

I check in, because I matter.

Even when no one sees.

Even when the world moves fast.

Even when I forget my name for a moment.

God remembers. My ancestors remember.

And now—I do too.

Closing Prayer: A Sacred Return to Self

Dear Divine Creator,

Thank You for the strength stitched into every wound,

for the soft places that didn't harden,

and for the grace that met me when I couldn't meet myself.

I pray for the soul reading this now

may they feel seen in their silence,

held in their healing,

and reminded that their presence is sacred.

Let their dreams stretch tall again.

Let their breath feel light again.

Let their voice come home to truth,

not performance. Not pressure. Just purpose.

Guide them back when they drift.

Whisper "you're enough" until they believe it.

Show them the power of choosing life again—

one quiet rise at a time.

Amen.

Asé.

And so it is.

Reminder !

You've Got This !

Just Walk In Love !

Resource List:

For the Journey Ahead

These people, pages, practices, and platforms can walk beside you as you rise—mentally, spiritually, creatively, and collectively. Keep what resonates. Share what heals.

Mental & Emotional Wellness

*   Therapy for Black Girls
    www.therapyforblackgirls.com
    A directory and podcast providing mental health support for Black women.

*   **Open Path Collective**
    www.openpathcollective.org
    Affordable therapy sessions with licensed professionals nationwide.

- **Black Men Heal**
www.blackmenheal.org
Providing access to mental health resources for Black men.

- **Black Man's Lab**
www.blackmanslab.org
A safe, intergenerational space fostering leadership, healing, and mentoring for Black men and boys.

- **National Suicide & Crisis Lifeline**
Dial 988 for 24/7 confidential support.

Spiritual Alignment & Mindfulness

- **Insight Timer**
www.insighttimer.com
Free meditations, music, and breath work tools to ease the mind and nourish the spirit.

- **The Nap Ministry**
  www.thenapministry.com
  A movement founded by Tricia Hersey,
  advocating rest as a form of resistance and
  spiritual reclamation.

- **All About Love** by bell hooks
  A transformative exploration of love, healing, and
  connection.

- **Sacred Woman** by Queen Afua
  A guide to physical and spiritual wellness through
  African ancestral teachings.

- **Journey to Selffullness** by Tassili Maat
  Available via: www.tassilisrawreality.com
  A sacred path to healing, forgiveness, and
  alignment with your higher self.

- **Our Daily Änkh** by Ahnkel Adam
  www.ourdailyankh.com
  A daily spiritual and ancestral guide rooted in universal African principles.
  IG: @ourdailyankh

Community, Finance & Creative Empowerment

- **FIYE Radio (FIYE 101.9 Atlanta Radio)**
  Uplifting voices and communities through music, interviews, and powerful stories.
  IG: @fiyeradio

- Email: info@fiyeradio.com | Phone: 678-471-2963
  www.fiyeradio.com

- **The Galaxy of Poets**
  A circle of poets, healers, and lyricists using words to liberate, laugh, and lead.
  IG: @thegalaxyofpoets

- **Dope Girls Grinding**- a production company creating experiences in all aspects of entertainment, from open mics to tours & everything in between while uplifting women on the grind along the way. www.dopegirlsgrinding.com

- **Phenomenal Hues**
  Financial education and wealth-building strategies for families, youth, and entrepreneurs.
  IG: @phenomenalhues

- **The Prison Brat Foundation**
  a 501 (c) (3) nonprofit organization. Keeping families together and kids safe. Serving children and families impacted by incarceration and homelessness.
  www.prisonbrats.com | Email: sundayjones@prisonbrats.com
  IG: @prisonbratfoundation

-

- **Lifestyle Legacy Coaching** with Sunday Jones
  Empowering lives, building legacies. Free consultations available.
  IG: @lifestylelegacycoaching
  Phone: 678-471-2963 | Email:
  sundayjonesislife@gmail.com

- **New Era Atlanta** — Community org empowering Black Atlanta & Detroit through connection and investment via IG: @neweraatlanta.

Reflection & Ritual

- Revisit the poem that cracked you open.

- Journal your truth in the margins.

- Look yourself in the mirror and say:
  "I am the revelation I've been waiting for."

This is not just a book. This is a mirror. A moment.
A map.

The Art of Rising: A Love Letter to My Becoming
Affirmations & Poetry for the Soul
by Sunday Jones

I didn't have this for my own journey so I wanted to
make sure that you did.
More by Sunday Jones

Your journey doesn't end here—this is just one
chapter of your rising.

Stay connected for:
  •   Upcoming books, including but not limited
to
Lost in Religion:
A Journey to Faith Beyond Labels
The Love They Deserve: Parenting Beyond Biology

Street Smarts & Survival:
Play It Right or Pay the Price

   •   Poetry performances & speaking
engagements
   •   Artist coaching, soul care retreats, and
lifestyle legacy mentorship

Book Sunday Jones for coaching or appearances
at:
sjones@dopegirlsgrinding.com
www.dopegirlsgrinding.com

Documentary "coming soon"
Follow her on IG @sundayjonesislife
sundayjonesislife@gmail.com